GUITARGAMES

LEARN GUITAR. READ MUSIC. FIGHT SPACE MONSTERS.

BY WILLIAM WILSON

ISBN 978-1-4234-9163-7

HAL•LEONARD®
CORPORATION

7777 W. BLUEMOUND RD. P.O. BOX 13819 MILWAUKEE, WI 53213

In Australia Contact:
Hal Leonard Australia Pty. Ltd.
4 Lentara Court
Cheltenham, Victoria, 3192 Australia
Email: ausadmin@halleonard.com.au

Visit Hal Leonard Online at
www.halleonard.com

CREDITS

Written and Illustrated by William Wilson.

Illustration backgrounds of space, messy office, evil laboratory, villain's lair, desert, and classroom, as well as game backgrounds for Birds of Fretopia, Chord Mines, Music Theory Blocks, Note Squish, and Woody Says by Cartoon Solutions.

Special Thanks to Matthew Lickona and Rick Ehrenfeld for their support and encouragement.

DEDICATION

To my wife Mary Ann, who named the Guitar Games' mascot Woody, and my sons Tad, Isaac, and Liam, who love him.

SYSTEM REQUIREMENTS

PC running Windows XP®, Windows Vista®, or Windows 7® with Internet Explorer® 5.5 or newer, and a CD-ROM drive.

Macintosh® computer running OS 10.4 (Tiger), OS 10.5 (Leopard), or OS 10.6 (Snow Leopard) with a CD-ROM drive.

HOW TO USE THE CD-ROM

After you insert the CD-ROM into your computer, you should see a window that displays all nine guitar games. If no window appears, you may need to search your computer for the Guitar Games disc. Once the window is open, double-click on any game to play it.

The Windows® and Macintosh® versions of Guitar Games are nearly identical; one small difference is the location of the quit button. Windows® users will see a quit button in the upper right hand corner of every game. Macintosh® users can quit by shutting the game window, selecting quit from the application window, or pressing Command-Q.

GUITAR GAMES FORUM AND RESOURCES

For support, discussion, and other resources, visit: **www.guitargamesbook.com**. The site is moderated by Guitar Games' author William Wilson and features a forum devoted to this book and CD-ROM.

TABLE OF CONTENTS

INTRODUCTION:
WHY GUITAR GAMES?

Often, even the largest and hardest tasks can be completed when broken down into smaller, easier steps. Learning to play the guitar is one such task. Taken as a whole, the process is monumental. On the purely physical side, a player must develop finger speed, strength, and independence, while at the same time learning to coordinate disparate hand motions. Meanwhile, on the mental side of things, a player must learn how to read music, and must memorize chords, scales, and songs. On top of all this, a player must develop an ear for music, and while physical skills are essential to mastering the guitar, it is the mental aspect—this knowledge of music—that informs a player's developing abilities. Breaking down the mental aspect of guitar playing into small and easy steps is what Guitar Games is all about.

Traditionally, the mental side of guitar playing has been dealt with in a conservatory setting, but this is far from ideal. Besides wading through courses in music theory, students are submitted to a battery of grueling ear training drills. Usually, all but a dedicated few leave out of boredom or frustration. The once-eager beginner might learn to read notes and recognize a few chords by ear, but will most likely not proceed further due to the dry, academic nature of the materials available. On top of this, many children with the potential to shine musically never get the chance because they lack appropriate resources for their age.

Enter *Guitar Games*. While these video games are fun and engaging, they also help students to begin mastering a wide range of challenging material. From ear training to note reading, and scales to key signatures, *Guitar Games* presents the material normally reserved for the conservatory setting in a way that is fun and accessible for any player, regardless of age or experience.

EXPLOSIVE CHORDS:
CHORD MINES

Learning chords is an important part of every guitarist's education. By playing chords, the guitar can accompany a singer or other instrument, which is easier, and in fact, more common than solo guitar playing. By learning chords first, guitarists are able to play music they enjoy in a relatively short amount of time. The process can be broken down into three steps: learning to read a chord chart, memorizing the chords, and playing those chords on the guitar. Reading a chord chart (step 1) is explained below, while the Chord Mines game focuses on memorizing chords (step 2). Practicing them (step 3) is up to you!

READING CHORD CHARTS

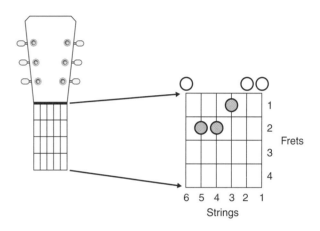

A chord chart is a grid showing the guitar's strings and frets (those metal things laying across the guitar neck). The vertical lines represent strings, and the horizontal lines represent frets (as shown above). This takes some getting used to, as the strings are not vertical when you actually play the guitar, but bear with it.

Circles on a chord chart show where to place your fingers and which strings to play. The filled circles represent your fingers. In the example above, for instance, you would have three fingers down: one finger on the fifth string at fret 2, one finger on fourth string at fret 2, and one finger on the third string at fret 1. (Hey, this sounds like I sunk your battleship!) The open circles at the top mean that an open string should be included in the strum. In the above example, for instance, the right hand should strum all six strings. If neither circle (closed or open) appears on a string, then the right hand should not strum that string. The following is our handy-dandy chord chart, which includes all the chords you'll need to play Chord Mines.

Guitar Games Chord Chart

 Finger

○ Open

E
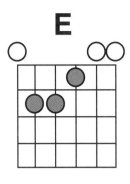

Em
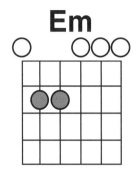

E7
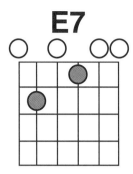

A
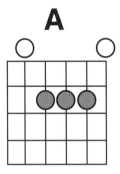

Am
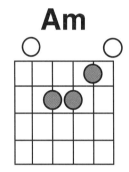

A7
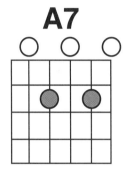

C
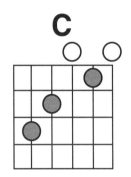

C7
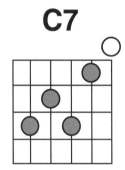

G
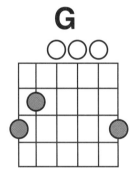

G7
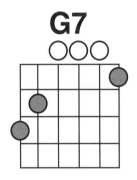

D
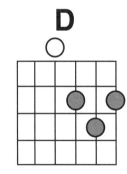

D7
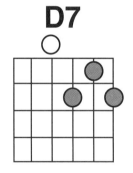

Dm
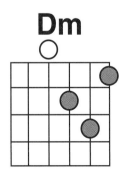

B7
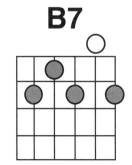

F
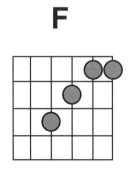

INSTRUCTIONS

Chord Mines is an arcade-style game that will teach you basic guitar chords. Learning chords is a great way to start playing guitar. Remember U2's famous expression: three chords and the truth!

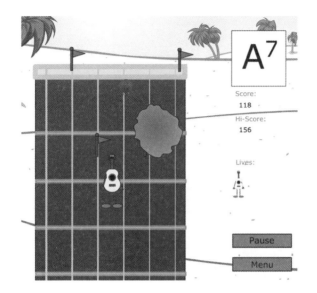 

In the Chord Mines game, you are Woody, a walking guitar, picking your way across a minefield that just happens to resemble a guitar fretboard. In the top corner of the screen, secret agents have placed a chord symbol, which is actually a secret code telling you which parts of the mine field are safe. Your job is to place flags on all the safe spots which coincide with those places you would place your fingers to make the given chord, plus any open strings. So, if the chord is "E," you will put flags in the following places: the sixth string (open), the fifth string (second fret), the fourth string (second fret), the third string (first fret), and the first and second strings (open)—just like the circles on the chord chart!

Woody can be moved by using the arrow keys on your keyboard. When you want to place a flag, just press the space bar.

Put a flag in the right place, and you get a point; finish the chord, and you get a big bonus! But, if a flag is put in the wrong spot, it sets off a mine. Setting off a mine causes a big explosion and you lose a life. Lose three lives, and the game is over. However, every time you get 250 points, you get a free life.

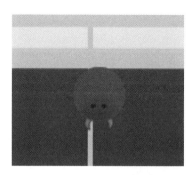

While placing the flags, watch out for danger! First along comes a spider; if you let him get too close, he'll bite you (not good)! After the spider come boulders to squish you (really not good). Both will cost you a life.

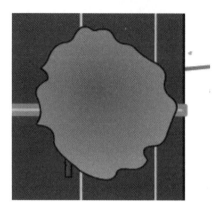

SETTINGS

The settings page allows you to choose between three levels of difficulty. The easy level includes chords that are easier to play and remember; the difficult level includes the dreaded F and B7 chords. The more difficult the chords you include, the higher your score.

To do:

If you're new to chords, have the chord sheet out and play Chord Mines on the easy setting. After playing once or twice, put the chord sheet away and see if you can play the chords from memory. When you feel comfortable with that, get out your guitar and try playing them for real. Repeat this for medium and difficult levels. Scores above 500 mean you are a chord master!

GAME SECRETS!

Try to stay away from the edge of the screen; that's where you're most likely to be hit by a boulder. When running away from a boulder, move up or down (rather than side to side) to get away from them quickly.

READING NOTES:
NOTE SQUISH & NOTE FISH

Every note has a name that comes from the musical alphabet, which runs from "A" to "G." Note names are like people's last names; they show that they are in a specific family. Many notes share the same name. For example, there are many E and F notes, and some are high and some are low. They share the same name because they sound similar. For instance, when a woman sings an "A" and a man sings an "A", we recognize the two sounds as the same pitch, even though the woman's sounds higher.

NOTES ON THE STAFF

The musical staff consists of five lines that tell us the names of the notes. It does NOT tell us where those notes are on the guitar. Take a look at the staff. The funny-looking thing at the beginning is called a *treble clef*. It was originally the letter G, but people have since fancied it up. See how it makes a target? Right in the middle of that target is a line that represents the note G. Now, if you go up or down one spot on the staff, you're simply moving up or down one letter in the musical alphabet. If you go down to the space below G, you get an F, and if you move to the space above G, you get an A. Why is it not an H? Remember, the musical alphabet only goes from A to G, so when you move above G, you start over again with A.

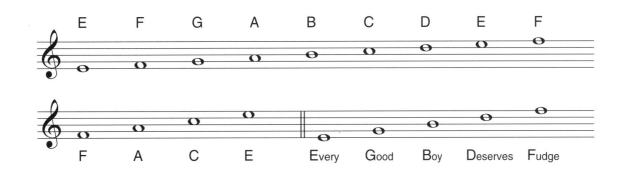

There are two memory tricks that make it easy to remember the names of the notes on the staff.

1. The notes in the spaces spell the word **F–A–C–E**, and F–A–C–E also rhymes with space.

2. The notes on the lines are the first letters to the sentence: **E**very **G**ood **B**oy **D**eserves **F**udge (or **E**very **G**ood **B**oy **D**oes **F**ine).

For notes above and below the staff, keep following the alphabet. Remember that the staff follows the musical alphabet A to G. Every time you move a spot on the staff, you move a spot in the alphabet. The short, temporary lines used when we move above or below the staff are called *ledger lines*.

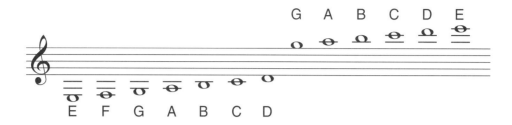

INSTRUCTIONS - NOTE SQUISH

Note Squish is a game designed to help guitarists get better at reading music. It does this by creating a strong connection between the name of a note and its location on the staff.

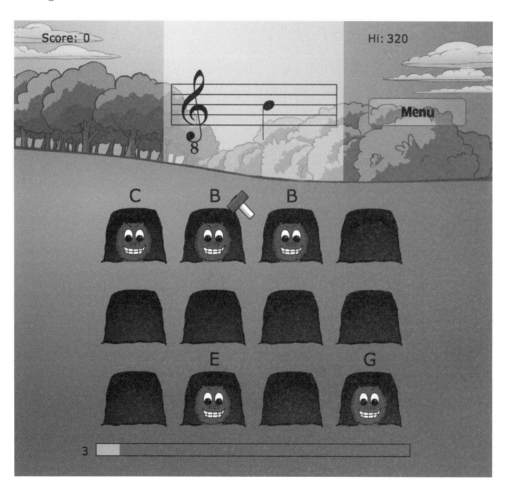

For this game, you need to focus on two parts of the screen. First, notice the staff at the top. Figure out the name of the note shown on the staff. Then, focus your attention on the moles below. Using the mouse, move the mallet over the mole who has the name of the correct note above their head. Click the mouse, and BLAM—you got him! Also, you can always hit a mole that says "Wild," and it will count as a correct note.

Be careful: if you click on the wrong mole, you'll lose points and he will ridicule you! The game starts by giving you 30 seconds. For every correct answer, you get two more seconds. For every incorrect answer, you lose two seconds. The time remaining is shown at the bottom of the screen.

SETTINGS

The settings page allows you to make the game easier or harder. You can choose to work on the notes below the staff, above the staff, or way above and below the staff.

To do:

Play Note Squish on the easy level first. Remember the memory tricks: FACE for the spaces and "Every Good Boy Deserves Fudge" for the lines. See if you can get a score above 400. Good luck!

GAME SECRETS!

Want a new note? Click on the treble clef, and presto, a new note will come up.

INSTRUCTIONS - NOTE FISH

Like Note Squish, Note Fish teaches the names of the notes on the staff. In the game, you are the note fish, and you swim by using the arrows on the keyboard.

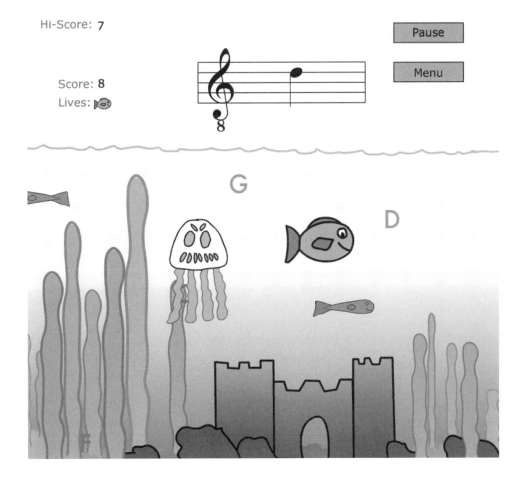

The note fish swims around eating the letters that fall into the water. You make him eat by pressing the spacebar. He can only eat a letter that matches the name of the note shown above the tank. For instance, if an "F" is shown, he can only eat the letter "F"—all the others will make him sick. Eating the correct letter earns him points, while eating the incorrect letter poisons him. When he earns fifty points, he gets an extra life.

Don't worry—there are other ways to die, too. (What fun is a game without some enemies?) Here they are:

Jellyfish
Pufferfish
Electric Eel

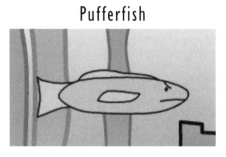 

Minnow

One other character you will see in the water is the minnow, but he won't hurt you—he's just out for a swim.

SETTINGS

The settings page gives you options as to which notes you want to be included in the game. Beginners should stick to level one. More advanced players can use any combination of levels shown. The higher levels give players more points.

To do:

Try to get a score above 300. That's one hungry fish!

GAME SECRETS!

When the eel comes, go immediately and hide behind the castle. Wait a minute, and the eel will go away. Hiding behind the castle will also help keep the pufferfish from chasing you. But watch out—the castle won't protect you from the jellyfish!

FINDING NOTES:
BIRDS OF FRETOPIA

THE OPEN STRINGS

Warning: More Silly Memory Tricks Ahead!

Let's learn the names of the open strings on the guitar. From low to high, they are E–A–D–G–B–E. To remember this, use the sentence: Elephants And Donkeys Grow Big Ears.

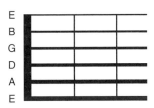

To do:

1. Play the open strings on the guitar as you say their names.

2. Play the open strings as you say: Elephants And Donkeys Grow Big Ears.

3. Draw your own elephant and donkey. (Really—it will help your memory. I know it sounds silly, but it works!)

THE BEE

Once upon a time, in a magical, musical land, the music alphabet made sense. There was one of each letter, A to G, and in between each letter was a sharp. It looked like this: A–A♯–B–B♯–C–C♯–D–D♯–E–E♯–F–F♯–G–G♯. The notes were kept in a huge fortress and looked as beautiful as they sounded. But one day, an evil musical bee decided that he wanted to steal the letters in his name: "B," "B♯," "E," and "E♯," in order to make a monument to himself. He climbed the castle wall and put the B♯ and E♯ in his bag. Little did he know that his buzzing would wake King

Muzo. The King awoke and saw the bee stealing the notes. He ran quickly to the fortress, but was too late. The bee saw him coming and flew away as fast as he could, taking B♯ and E♯ with him. The King was able to save B and E, but B♯ and E♯ were gone forever. To this day, our musical alphabet reads A–A♯–B–C–C♯–D–D♯–E–F–F♯–G–G♯.

A–A#–B–C–C#–D–D#–E–F–F#–G–G#

Great story, right? Okay, so I'm no Brothers Grimm. The point is this: there is no B or E sharp. Once B# and E# are removed, the notes fit neatly onto the frets. Each piece of the musical alphabet (A–A#–B–C–C#, etc.) corresponds to one fret. The open fifth string is A. Look at the musical alphabet shown above, and find A. Immediately following A in the musical alphabet is A#. Therefore, the first fret on the fifth string is A#. The second fret is B, the third is C, the fourth is C#, the fifth is D, and on and on up the post-bee musical alphabet.

That's it! You now have the tools to find the notes up and down the neck. Just go to an open string (Elephants And Donkeys Grow Big Ears) and move up the musical alphabet to find the note for any fret.

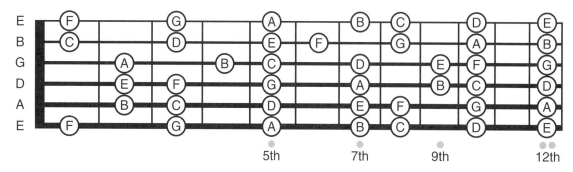

Diagram of Note Names on Guitar Neck

INSTRUCTIONS

Your mission: capture the alien birds that are tagged for the intergalactic guitar show. (Oh yeah, and master the fretboard in the process.)

In this game, there is a fretboard display, and your job is to figure out the name of the note for the location marked with a red circle. Then, shoot the bird with the matching note name. You move the target with the mouse and shoot by clicking.

There are three types of birds:

Fiordiligi   Dorabella   Despina

 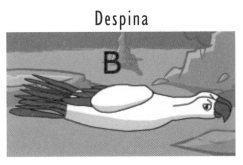

If you zap the correct bird, you get points and extra time on the timer. If you zap the wrong bird, you lose points and time. After each correct answer, a new note will be shown on the fretboard.

If you see a "Wild" or a UFO, zap them! It will count the same as a correct answer.

SETTINGS

Use the settings page to choose which strings and frets to include in the game. This is handy if you're having trouble with the notes in only one area, or if you are just learning and only know the notes on the first few strings. You can choose strings one through six or any combination you desire. You can also select a range of frets to use, from the whole fretboard to one position to one fret.

SCORING

Points are awarded depending on the settings you choose. The more strings you choose and the higher the position you select, the more points you get per zap. The high positions of the guitar neck (anything above the fifth fret) are harder to learn, so they merit a few extra points.

To do:

Play Birds of Fretopia with just the first three frets of the first string. In the next game, move up to two strings, then three, four, five, and finally all six. When you are comfortable with those, start adding additional frets, one by one. When you get a score above 1000, you are a fretboard master!

GAME SECRETS!

Are all the birds the wrong letter? Click on the double dots at the twelfth fret, and all the birds will disappear, clearing the way for a bird with the letter you need.

FROM PAGE TO FRET:
FRET TESTER

Let's review what you've learned so far. First, we studied how to name the notes on the staff. For the lines of the staff, use the sentence "Every Good Boy Deserves Fudge," and for the spaces, remember the word "FACE." For notes above and below the staff (on ledger lines), keep in mind that the notes are alphabetical: move up or down one spot on the staff, and you are moving up or down one letter name.

Second, we learned how to find notes on the guitar. The open strings (from low to high) are E–A–D–G–B–E, which can be remembered with the phrase "Elephants And Donkeys Grow Big Ears." Combine this with the knowledge that each fret moves up or down one spot in the musical alphabet, and you can find any note name. For example, to find the note located at the sixth fret on the second string, start with B (second string open) and move up the musical alphabet six spots: C–1, C#–2, D–3, D#–4, E–5, F–6. Therefore, the note is F.

MORE LANDMARKS

If you start with the open strings (Elephants And Donkeys Grow Big Ears) and move your way up the fretboard, finding notes in the higher positions can be a little time-consuming. A good way to speed up the process is to learn other starting points. By memorizing the note names on the fifth, tenth, and twelfth frets, you can greatly reduce the time it takes to find notes. The process is still the same: start with a note you know, and move up one spot in the musical alphabet for each fret.

The notes on the fifth fret, from the sixth string to the first, are A–D–G–C–E–A, which can be remembered by learning the sentence "Ants Drive Go Carts Every Afternoon." The notes at the tenth fret, from the sixth string to the first, are D–G–C–F–A–D, which can be remembered by learning the sentence "Dogs Get Cold Fast After Dark. The twelfth fret, often shown with double dots, is the spot where the note's names repeat on that string. So, you can use "Elephants And Donkeys Grow Big Ears" just as you did for the open strings. Use these memory tricks as you make your way up the fretboard, and you'll save time.

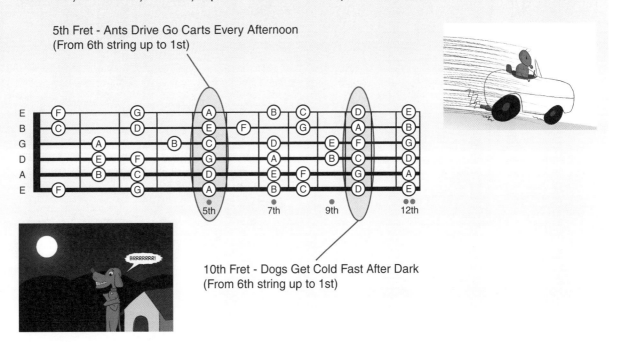

5th Fret - Ants Drive Go Carts Every Afternoon
(From 6th string up to 1st)

10th Fret - Dogs Get Cold Fast After Dark
(From 6th string up to 1st)

SHARPS AND FLATS

Sharp   Flat

Every sharp could also be described as a flat. If you think of a sharp as one fret higher than a note, a flat is just one fret lower than a note. For example, F♯ is one fret higher than F, and G♭ is one fret lower than G, but they're both the same note!

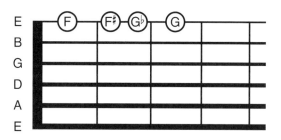

Have you ever wondered why there are sharps and flats? Why not use letter names "A" through "L" instead? The answer comes from our use of scales and keys. Most music doesn't normally use all twelve possible notes at once—usually just seven that fit well together. This grouping of seven notes is called a *key*. Therefore, there are only seven note names (A to G), and every key uses some form of the seven letter names. It might be a sharp or flat version, but every key has just one of each letter name.

FROM THE STAFF TO THE FRETBOARD

In this section, we connect finding notes on the staff to finding them on the guitar. We develop the ability to look at a note on the staff and be able to say exactly where it is on the guitar. For example, right now you know that the first string is an E. But, which E? Is it the one on the top or the bottom of the staff? The following chart shows the relationship between the staff and the fretboard. Study it carefully and connect your knowledge of the staff to the names on the fretboard. If you've played Note Squish and Note Fish, you should be quick at naming the notes on the staff. Birds of Fretopia should have taught you the note names on the fretboard. Fret Tester will tie these both together. When you master it, you'll be able to see a note on the staff and immediately find its location on the fretboard. Start with learning the first position, and then move on to the whole neck.

Guitar Games First Position Chart

Guitar Games Guitar Fretboard Chart

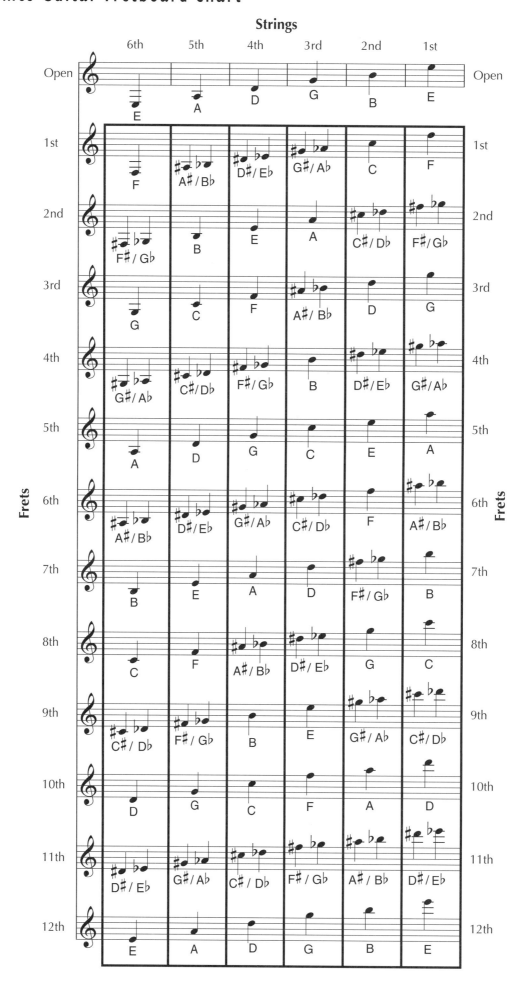

INSTRUCTIONS

Fret Tester helps you connect the location on the staff to the location on the guitar. A note is shown at the top of the game; you must click on the fret corresponding to the note shown. If it is a note that corresponds to an open string, click on the nut of the correct string (see the arrow with the word "Open"). If you click on the correct fret, you get points; if you click on an incorrect fret, you lose points. If you make a mistake, the "show answer" button appears; this will show you the correct location if you click on it.

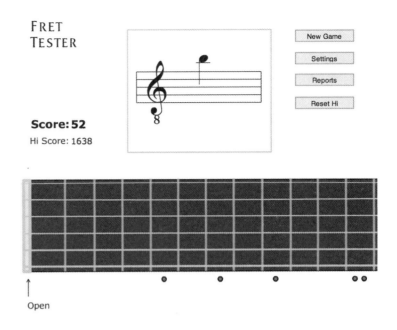

FRET TESTER

Score: 52
Hi Score: 1638

New Game

Settings

Reports

Reset Hi

↑
Open

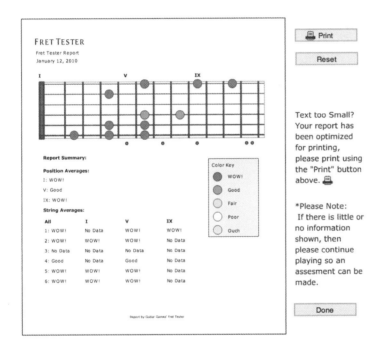

REPORTS

Reports are a great way to chart your progress with Fret Tester. They can help pinpoint problem areas and gauge improvement. Teachers love them, since students can print them out and bring them to lessons to show their progress. Students benefit from reports because they help them complete their goals. Reports show your strength on the fretboard and summarize each position and string. Dots are placed on the fretboard, showing your strengths and weaknesses. Red dots mean you have done well for that location and blue dots signify an area still needs work.

SETTINGS

Use the settings page to choose which strings and positions to include in the game. If you have trouble with the notes in only one area, select that area in the settings page to focus your efforts. You can choose strings one through six or any combination you desire. Frets are grouped into three areas: first to fourth, fifth to eighth, and ninth to twelfth. Start by mastering each of these three positions, and then combine them for a greater challenge. The settings page also allows you to include sharps and/or flats.

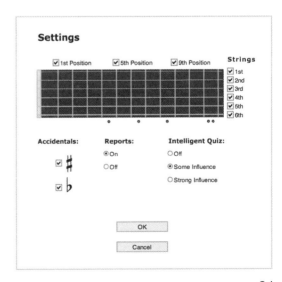

INTELLIGENT QUIZ MODE

Intelligent Quiz Mode drastically speeds up the learning process. While in Intelligent Quiz Mode, Fret Tester emphasizes areas of the neck where you have made mistakes. This means you spend less time going over stuff you already know and more time learning new material. Intelligent Quiz Mode has three levels of influence: strong influence, some influence, or no influence (off). You can select the level of influence on the settings page. The different levels of influence allow users to include various amounts of review in the game. Strong influence minimizes the amount of review.

SCORING

The more strings, positions, and notes you include in the Settings page (don't forget sharps and flats), the more points you get per click. Also, notes in fifth position are worth twice the notes in first position, and the notes in ninth position are worth three times the notes in first position.

To do:

As with Birds of Fretopia, it's best to start small and build. Set the game to one or two strings in one position. Play with those until the report shows you have mastered them (all red dots). Then, add sharps and flats. When those are also mastered, increase the number of strings. When you have one position mastered, add another one. Soon, you'll have the whole fretboard down! As of this printing, the all-time high score for Fret Tester is an amazing 121,342 scored by Marinella Casertano of Sicily. Wow!

KEY SIGNATURES ARE FUN:
KEY HUNT

KEYS AND KEY SIGNATURES

What is a key?

A key is a collection of seven notes that sound like they belong together. Over many centuries, musicians found they were using the same groups of notes over and over. Many melodies (songs) contained the same seven notes spread throughout the song. Some smart musicians decided they should group these notes together, and the concept of the key was born. However, not all seven notes in a key were used equally. Musicians found that songs often started and ended on certain notes, while others were only used sparingly. The note that was used the most is what we now call the *root* note (also known as the *tonic*). When it is played, it gives the listener a sense of "coming home" or resolution, making the song sound complete. The root note is how we name a key, since all the other notes gravitate towards it.

What is a scale?

A scale is produced when you play all the notes in a key in order. For example, if you play the notes in the key of G major, you get: G–A–B–C–D–E–F♯.

Why are scales called major or minor?

When musicians began grouping notes together into keys and scales, they found that different groups of notes produce a different sound. A *major* scale refers to a certain type of scale—one which is usually associated with happy, joyful music. Major scales are so common that often the word "major" is left out when naming the scale. For instance, the "Key of C Major" is the same as saying the "Key of C." Another common type of scale is a *minor* scale; this scale contains different notes than a major scale and produces a sad, melancholy sound. For example, a G minor scale contains the notes G–A–B♭–C–D–E♭–F–G. Try playing it on your guitar. Then, play G major (G–A–B–C–D–E–F♯–G). Can you hear the difference?

How do you find the notes within a key?

Every type of key/scale is made from a unique blueprint. All major scales follow a specific pattern of whole steps and half steps (see sidebar on whole steps and half steps on page 24). Major scales are all built from the following pattern:

```
      Whole Whole  Half  Whole Whole Whole  Half
G  -  A  -  B  -  C  -  D  -  E  - F♯ -  G
```

Root note, up a whole step, up another whole step, up a half step, up a whole step, up another whole step, up one more whole step, and finish up with a half step. This is often abbreviated WWHWWWH, where W stands for whole step and H stands for half step.

Try this for the key of G, and you should get G–A–B–C–D–E–F♯–G. (The last G note is actually the start of another octave. Notes in different octaves have the same name and sound the same, only higher or lower.) But, using this pattern can be a lot of work, so it's not really practical for figuring out keys quickly. This is why keys are more often memorized using key signatures.

WHAT ARE WHOLE STEPS AND HALF STEPS?

A whole step is the basic distance between two notes (like F to G), which are two frets apart on the guitar. A half step is half that distance, or one fret. Don't forget that there is a sharp (or flat) between most letter names in the musical alphabet (except for the ones stolen by the bee!).

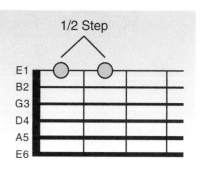

What are key signatures?

Ever notice all those funny sharps or flats at the beginning of a piece of music? They're the ones you're supposed to remember and use throughout the entire piece. Sometimes, there are a couple of sharps; other times, you see some flats. That grouping of sharps or flats is called a *key signature*. It's kind of like the thumbprint for a key. The key of G major, for instance, has a key signature with one sharp: F♯.

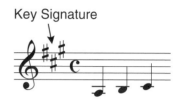

Key Signature

No other major key has that signature—only G major. Now, if you know a key's signature, you can figure out its corresponding scale. If we have the key of G, and know that its signature is F♯, then we know that the scale contains the notes G–A–B–C–D–E–F♯–G. In other words, it has one of each letter name (A through G), and accidentals (sharps or flats) in the signature are thrown in too. Here's another example: B♭ ("B-flat"). It has a key signature with two flats: B♭ and E♭. So, its scale is B♭–C–D–E♭–F–G–A–B♭. Also notice that key signatures never use both sharps AND flats; it's always either sharps OR flats. This will be crucial in your efforts to remember them.

C MAJOR

The key of C major has no sharps or flats. Therefore, its scale is spelled C–D–E–F–G–A–B–C. It doesn't fit into our memory tricks for sharps or flats since it doesn't have any!

HOW TO MEMORIZE KEY SIGNATURES

First, let's look at the sharp keys:

G: F♯

D: F♯–C♯

A: F♯–C♯–G♯

E: F♯–C♯–G♯–D♯

B: F♯–C♯–G♯–D♯–A♯

F♯: F♯–C♯–G♯–D♯–A♯–E♯

C♯: F♯–C♯–G♯–D♯–A♯–E♯–B♯ (ugly!)

Notice a pattern here? First off, the sharps appear in a certain order. You will never see a key signature with only A♯; the signature will always start with F♯, and proceed through the order of the sharps until it gets to A♯. So, if you know the number of sharps in a key (e.g., E has 4), and you know the order of sharps, then you know what sharps that key has (E has F♯ C♯ G♯ D♯). The pattern can be remembered by using the device: Fat Cats Go Down Alleys Eating Bananas.

But wait...there's more! Notice the relationship between the last sharp in a key and the key name. For example, F♯ is the last sharp in the key of G, C♯ is the last sharp in the key of D, G♯ is the last sharp in the key of A, and etc. Do you see the pattern? Yes, the last sharp is always one half step below the name! F♯ is one below G, C♯ is one below D, and G♯ is one below A (in the musical alphabet). So what, you ask. Well, given that sharps appear in a certain order, and we know what the last sharp in a signature is going to be, we can easily remember the signature. Take B as an example. What is one half step below B? A♯ (If you got that wrong, we're in trouble). Now, go in the order of sharps until you get to A♯: Fat Cats Go Down And, or F♯–C♯–G♯–D♯–A♯. There it is!

Key of B

A **A♯ B** C C♯ D D♯ E F F♯ G G♯

One note below tells you the last note in the key signature.

F♯ C♯ G♯ D♯ **A♯** E♯ B♯

Follow the order of sharps until you get to that note.

Now for flats. You know, they look like the letter "b," and make you want to throw your guitar out the window. Don't despair; help is on the way. Here are the flat key signatures:

F: B♭

B♭: B♭ E♭

E♭: B♭ E♭ A♭

A♭: B♭ E♭ A♭ D♭

D♭: B♭ E♭ A♭ D♭ G♭

G♭: B♭ E♭ A♭ D♭ G♭ C♭

C♭: B♭ E♭ A♭ D♭ G♭ C♭ F♭ (very ugly!)

Once again, we have a pattern, and as with the sharps, we have an order for the flats. Compare the order of flats to the order of sharps. Notice any similarities? It may not be obvious at first glance, but the order of flats is the same as the order of sharps, but backwards. So, you could think "Bananas Eating Alleys Down Go Cats Fat" (just a little joke). A better way to remember them is to think of the order as the word "BEAD" and then add "gcf." This works, even though it's not quite as convenient as the device for the sharps.

KEY OF F

The trick for remembering flat keys requires the key to have at least two flats. F has only one flat, so you'll just have to remember that the key signature for F is B♭.

The trick where you look at the last ♯ doesn't work with the flats. There is another trick though, that works with all the flat keys (except F—see sidebar). Take a look at the second to last flat for any flat key. Compare the second to last flat to the name of the key. For B♭, it's B♭; for E♭, it's E♭; for A♭, it's A♭, and etc. Very convenient, huh? Now, to find the key signature for a flat key, all you have to do is go in the order of flats until you find to the name of the key and then go one further. Take G♭, for example. Think "BEAD" plus "gcf." You go until you reach the G♭—that's B♭–E♭–A♭–D♭–G♭—then add one more from the order, and you get B♭–E♭–A♭–D♭–G♭–C♭. That way, G♭ is the second to last flat, which matches the pattern.

Key of G♭

Follow the order of flats until you get to the key name.

B♭ E♭ A♭ D♭ **G**♭ C♭ F♭

Go one spot further in the order to get the full signature.

B♭ E♭ A♭ D♭ G♭ **C**♭ F♭

INSTRUCTIONS

Key Hunt is an arcade-style game that teaches key signatures. In the game, you play Woody the Guitar Guy, an intrepid explorer searching for the lost keys of Muzo Land. You move through Muzo Land with the arrow keys on your keyboard and use the space bar (or up arrow) to jump. The down arrow makes you kneel and cover your eyes, which might come in handy should any dangerous acid drop from the sky (hint, hint).

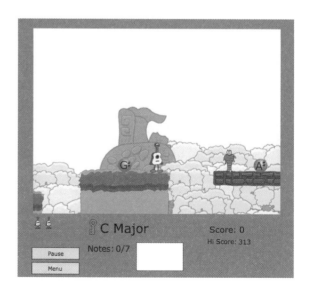

GAME TIP!

You will need to get really good at jumping, for there are many deep caverns in Muzo Land. To take a longer jump, continue to hold the right or left arrow down as you jump (depending on which way you are headed). If you've jumped too far, you can shorten your jump by pushing the arrow in the opposite direction while you're in the air.

On the bottom of the screen, you'll notice the name of a key. Each level will have its own key (so make sure you check when you pass a level!). Throughout the level, you will see the lost note jewels of Muzo Land, each with a miraculous note name etched on it.

You want to collect all the notes in the key shown. Be careful though: if you collect a note jewel with a note name not in the key shown, it will poison you. For instance, a G♯ would not be a choice if the key shown was C major. One touch of its deadly toxins, and you are a goner. When you collect a note, it will appear in your note collection box.

In the example on the right, you can see that three out of seven notes were collected (since each key has seven unique notes), and that you collected the notes C, D, and F. When you collect all the notes, the magic Muzo key will appear. It will be hidden somewhere in the level, and you need to find it (that's the "hunt" part of the "Key Hunt" game) to proceed to the next level.

Remember: it won't appear until you find all seven notes in the key. If you get to the end of the level without finding all seven notes and the magic key, you will see a closed door. This means that you still need to collect the key. When you do, the door will open.

There are twelve levels in all and they get progressively harder. Along the way, you'll meet many obstacles. When you see a termite, make sure to stomp it. After all, you are made of wood!

To do:

Try playing Key Hunt. For those of you who didn't spend your childhood zombie-eyed in front of a video game console, Key Hunt can be pretty hard. Non-gamers might make some flash cards with the name of a key on the front and the key signature on the back. Make a game out of it by seeing how fast you can get through the whole set.

GAME SECRETS!

Want to try out the higher levels or work on the harder keys? Hold down a number key for the level you want (e.g., for level 5, hold down the number 5) as you click on the start button on the opening page (the green page with the big key).

There are lots of tricks for the game itself. First, the spikes only hurt you when you land on them; otherwise, you can walk right through them. Second, there are two levels you don't even need a key to exit. Look for an easy way out on one level in the sky and one on land in another.

MUSIC THEORY 101:
EAR TESTER & MUSIC THEORY BLOCKS

New to music theory? Let's get you started with intervals. No, they're not exciting, but we put the "fun" in FUNdamentals! (Bad pun. Very bad pun.)

INTRODUCING INTERVALS

What is an interval? An *interval* is the distance between two notes. The term is used to describe two notes played together (*harmonic interval*), or one after the other (*melodic interval*).

Try this: play the following two notes together:

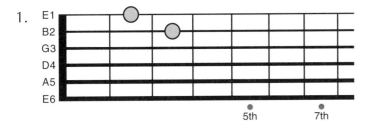

Write down a description of what you hear. Use any adjectives that apply: serene, peaceful, solid, military-like, ugly, sad, harsh, pretty, happy, etc.—whatever pops into your mind. It could also be a song name that pops into your head. You might think: "hey, that's the way 'Disco Inferno' starts!" Write that down.

Repeat for the following two intervals:

2.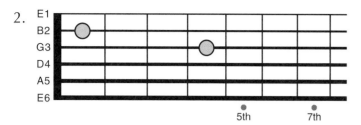

3.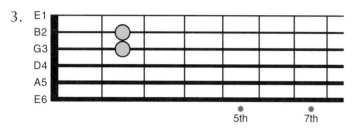

What do you notice about the similarities and differences of your descriptions? Are any two the same? Would it surprise you to know that the first and third are the same interval? Even though they don't involve the same notes, they sound similar because in each case, the notes are the same distance apart. Every interval has its own sound. If you want a certain sound, you can use a specific interval to get that sound. For instance, the minor 2nd interval is usually described as tense and harsh. John Williams made use of this interval in his theme from the movie *Jaws*, and it helped raise the tension before the shark actually attacked. These intervals are useful things! Let's get into the nuts and bolts.

FIGURING OUT INTERVALS

There are several methods of describing the distance between two notes. You could measure a given interval in half steps or frets. (For more on half steps, see earlier sidebar "What are whole steps and half steps?" on page 24.) Take C up to B: it is eleven half steps from one note to the other, but counting all these half steps is not practical. Fortunately, there's a better and more useful way.

Instead of naming intervals by half steps, we're going to measure them by letter distance. Let's take C to E. Count the number of letters from C to E, including C as 1. You'll get: C–1, D–2, E–3. Therefore, since there are three letters, we say that C to E is a 3rd. That's much simpler. We call this an interval's quantity. But wait—there's a problem. What if we did the same thing for C to E♭? There are still just three letters, so C to E♭ is also a 3rd. But clearly, the sound it makes is not the same as the 3rd made by C to E. A ha! That's where an interval's quality comes in.

C–D–E

Did you ever study astronomy? Remember Ursa Major and Ursa Minor? Major was the big one and minor was the small. The same thing is true in music. C to E is a major 3rd, and C to E♭ is a minor 3rd. The major label indicates it is the bigger of the two. That is, there are more half steps in the major 3rd than in the minor 3rd.

There are also three other types of intervals: perfect, augmented, and diminished. The perfect intervals (4ths, 5ths, and 8th) don't normally have a big or small version, so we refer to them as perfect 4ths, perfect 5ths, and perfect 8ths. To be clear: there is no such thing as a major 4th, major 5th, or major 8th. Way back in the early days of harmony (think Middle Ages), these intervals were considered better sounding, while the others were thought of as more dissonant (including the major 3rd!) A diminished interval is one half step smaller than a minor or perfect interval, and the augmented is one half step larger than a major or perfect interval. Distinctions such as these refer to the interval's quality.

Unfortunately, naming intervals by just counting letter names (as we did above) only works out neatly when you start on the note C. If you start on another note, you need to count up within that note's key. Let's take D as an example. To find a major 3rd above D, count up the D major scale: D–1, E–2, F♯–3. So, D to F♯ is a major 3rd. (For a review of how to find the notes in a scale, read the section on key signatures.)

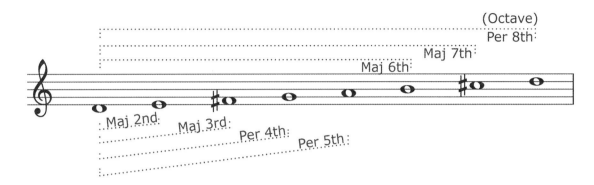

All intervals within a major scale are major or perfect intervals. (By the way, that's where the interval name comes from.) So, the distance from the first note of a major scale to the second is a major 2nd. The distance from the first note in a major scale to the third is a major 3rd. The distance from the first note in a major scale to the fourth is a perfect 4th, and on and on up the scale. In this way, if you know your major scales, you can easily find any interval. Always count the letter names to double check that you've done things correctly. For example, if you are looking for a major 3rd above D and come up with G♭, that's incorrect, since four letter names are involved (D–E–F–G), not three. A 3rd interval will always involve three note names.

What about minor, diminished, and augmented intervals? They are not found in the major scale. To find these intervals, first find the major or perfect version of the interval, and then adjust by half steps. As an example, let's find a minor 3rd above D. First, we find the major 3rd above D: D–1, E–2, F♯–3. A major 3rd above D is F♯. Since we know a minor 3rd is one half step smaller than a major 3rd, we just lower the F♯ to an F, and there's our minor 3rd: D to F. Augmented intervals are one half step larger that major or perfect intervals, and diminished intervals are one half step smaller than minor or perfect intervals, and can be found using the same process.

Hey, you're still awake! You are on your way to becoming a theory master. Learning intervals is the first step towards understanding scales, chords, and a lot more. Fill out the interval worksheet on pages 32 and 33. Simply play each example and write a description for each, just as we did at the beginning of this section. When you've finished, you'll have a description of every interval and be ready to play Ear Tester.

Interval Worksheet

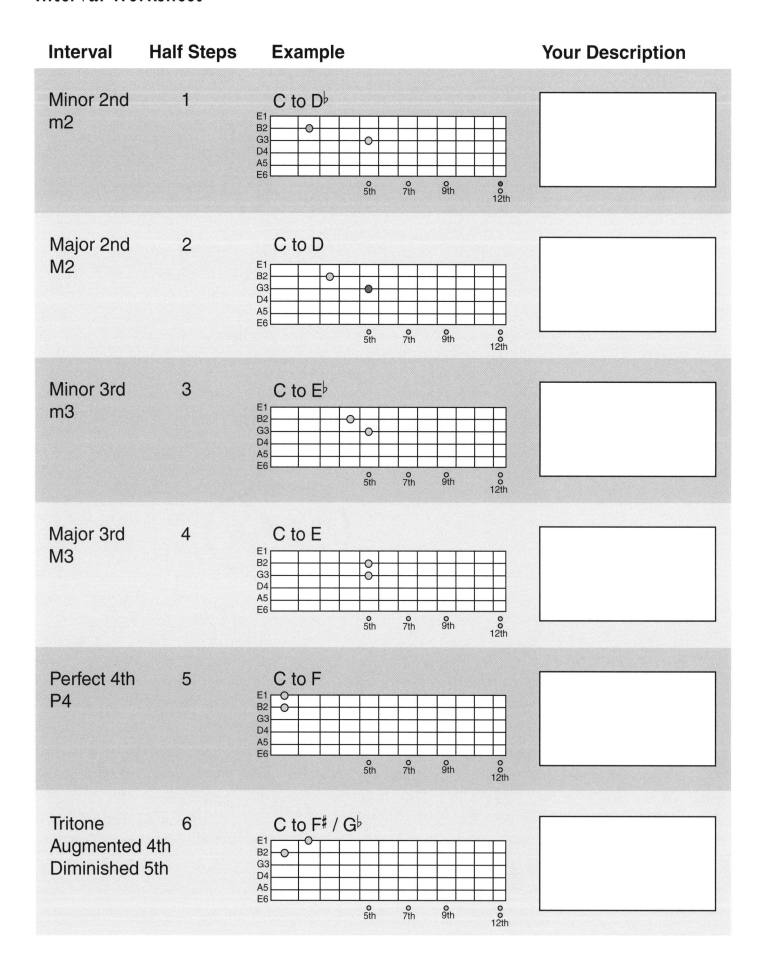

Interval	Half Steps	Example	Your Description
Minor 2nd m2	1	C to D♭	
Major 2nd M2	2	C to D	
Minor 3rd m3	3	C to E♭	
Major 3rd M3	4	C to E	
Perfect 4th P4	5	C to F	
Tritone Augmented 4th Diminished 5th	6	C to F♯ / G♭	

Interval	Half Steps	Example	Your Description

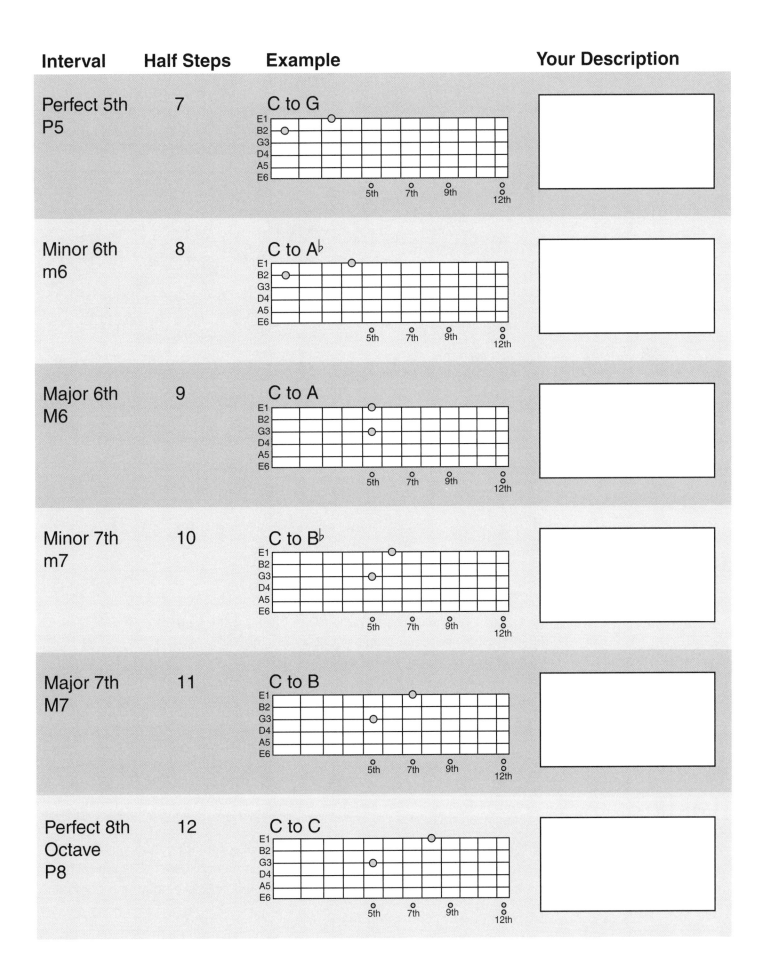

33

INSTRUCTIONS - EAR TESTER

Ear Tester is an ear training game designed to help you identify intervals and chords just by hearing them. First, pick what type of ear training you want to do: intervals, triads (another name for simple chords), or seventh chords (larger extended chords). If you just finished the last section, pick intervals. If you're already a theory guru, try seventh chords for a challenge. You will hear an example played. Simply click on the circle that corresponds to what you hear, and that's it. If you should miss one, a "Show Answer" button will appear to help. If have your filled-out interval worksheet with you, listen to the interval, run through your descriptions until you find a match, and click on that interval. In this way, you'll get to know how each interval sounds.

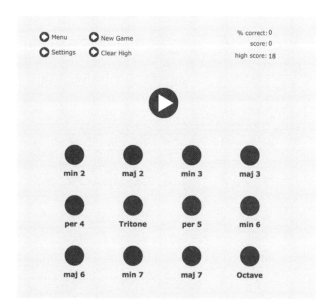

SETTINGS

The Settings page allows for extensive customization. You can include more or fewer choices. For example, say you need to brush up on hearing the difference between minor and major chords. Go to settings. For a greater ear training challenge, try deselecting the "Play Separate" check box. You will then only hear the examples played with all notes together (harmonic intervals). This is challenging ear training!

SCORING

Points are awarded depending on the settings you choose and the type of ear training (intervals, triads, or sevenths). Harder settings, such as choosing more intervals, give you a higher score. Also notice the "% correct" field. If you have a higher percentage of correct answers, you'll get more points per correct answer.

Points are taken away for each incorrect answer, and your "% correct" decreases. Should your percentage correct get too low for your liking, click on "New Game" to start fresh.

To do:

1. If you haven't already, finish the interval worksheet.

2. Play the game with minor 3rds and major 3rds. When you can tell the difference between them, add others.

3. Look for intervals that sound similar, like perfect 4ths and perfect 5ths. Play the game with only these intervals selected until you can tell them apart.

BUILDING CHORDS WITH INTERVALS

Intervals are the building blocks of music, but to build with them, you need a blueprint. Chords are made up of specific combinations of intervals. The most common type of chord is a triad, so named because it contains three different notes. The most common triad is the major chord. (It is so common that usually it is not included in a chord name—e.g., a D chord is actually a D major chord.) To

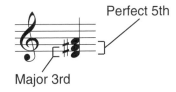

build a major chord, you need three notes: the root, a major 3rd above the root, and a perfect 5th above the root. Every major chord is built according to that blueprint. For example, a D major chord would include a D, the note a major 3rd above D, and the note a perfect 5th above D. Using your knowledge from the interval section, you know that a major 3rd above D is F♯ and a perfect 5th above D is A. Therefore, a D major chord is made up of the notes D, F♯, and A. By following this blueprint for a major chord, you can create a chord in any key. Let's take an E major chord. It would include E, a major 3rd above, which is G♯, and a perfect 5th above E, which is B, giving you E–G♯–B.

Each type of chord has its own blueprint. For instance, a minor chord includes a minor 3rd and a perfect 5th. If you were to build one starting on D, you would get the notes D, F, and A. By following the minor chord blueprint, you build a minor chord from any root note. The following diagram shows the blueprint for five basic chords: major, minor, augmented, diminished, and dominant 7th chords.

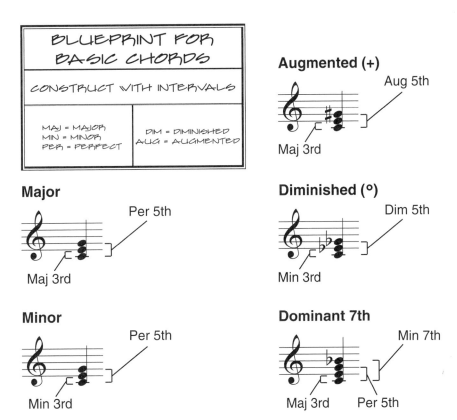

Most guitar chords contain four, five, or six notes. Look back to the Guitar Games chord chart to see the most common chords. Where do these chords come from? Why don't they have just three notes like the examples above? Actually, they do. They have only three unique notes. The rest of the notes are doubled in different octaves. Take a D major chord, for example. On the guitar, from low to high, we play the notes D, A, D, and F#. Even though there are four notes being played, only three are unique; the D (root note) is doubled. Also, notice that the notes are in a different order. Instead of D, F#, and A, they appear in our guitar chord as D, A, D, and F#. That's okay too; notes in a chord can be placed in any order.

SEVENTH CHORDS

In the "Blueprint for Basic Chords," there is one chord called a "dominant 7th." It has four notes instead of three. It's built up from a major 3rd and perfect 5th like a major chord, but it also adds a minor 7th as well. Just like triads, there are different kinds of seventh chords. When played on the guitar, seventh chords contain fewer doubled notes than major chords.

INSTRUCTIONS - MUSIC THEORY BLOCKS

Music Theory Blocks is a puzzle game where you try to group together different musical elements. First, choose what you want to work on: intervals, chords, or scales. Once you choose from these categories, you can select a specific type (e.g., "major 2nd," "Phrygian," etc.). Then, click on "Start."

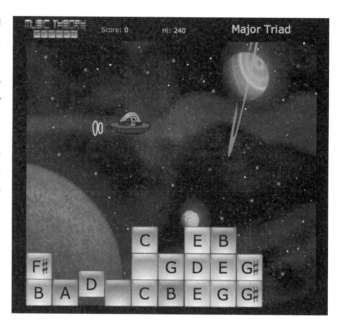

Your job is to put blocks together that form the type of interval, chord, or scale you selected. Let's say you selected major 3rds; you need to group major 3rds together. You could put C next to E, D next to F#, E next to G#, etc. (Review the Music Theory 101 section for how to spell intervals.) The major 3rd could be in any key and in any position so long as the notes were in the correct order. Blocks fall from the top to the bottom. Each block has a note name on it. You can move the blocks using the arrow keys.

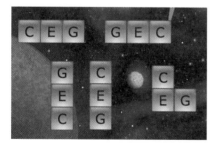

When you put the correct blocks together, you receive points and the blocks disappear. You'll then hear a demonstration of the sound created (e.g., a major 3rd, major scale, etc.). The game ends when a block stack reaches the top.

GAME SECRETS!

It pays to be organized. By stacking blocks of the same note name together, they're easier to find.

Level

There are three difficulty levels: easy, medium, and hard. The easy level tends to favor easier keys like C, D, E, F, G, and A. As the difficulty increases, more difficult keys are added, including some using double sharps and double flats.

UFO

Every once in a while, a UFO will fly by. This signals that the game is speeding up. (That, or the invasion is about to begin!)

To do:

Start by playing the game with the easiest interval: the major 2nd. This will get you used to the game. Then move on to 3rds and 5ths, which are used a lot in chords. After you're comfortable with them, play with all the different chords shown in the blueprint for basic chords (major, minor, diminished, augmented, and 7th).

MUSIC THEORY CALCULATOR

Within the Music Theory Blocks game, there is a music theory calculator. It can be used to compute intervals, chords, and scales. When you first start learning music theory, it can be difficult to spell intervals and chords correctly. Use the music theory calculator to check your work.

To access the calculator, click on the calculator icon in the upper right hand corner of the game, or click on the "Theory Calc" button on the opening screen.

The calculator is divided into three sections: Chords, Scales, and Intervals. Within each section, there are two drop-down menus: one to choose the root and one to choose the type (e.g., major chord, minor scale, perfect 5th, etc.). After selecting from these menus, click the "Answer" button, and the correct note names will appear in the box below.

MUSIC MELODY & MEMORY MADNESS:
WOODY SAYS

A MUSICAL COPYCAT GAME

The guitar is a visual instrument. Just look at it: the strings and frets form a big grid. But along with this visual nature comes certain problems—namely, the fact that you can play the instrument without thinking of what sound you want to produce. A rock player could simply put their fingers on the right fret from the right pattern and think he is making music. Evan a classical guitarist might be able to read and play all the right notes without regard for what sounds they produce. But ultimately, playing notes from a pattern or a page won't make beautiful, inspiring music. A connection must be made between where the notes are on the guitar and what they sound like. Enter Woody Says, a musical copycat game that creates this connection.

A copycat game is one where you mimic what appears on the screen. A melody is played on the guitar fretboard, and you echo it back by clicking on the correct frets. By doing this over and over, you create an association between the sounds produced and the distances on the guitar fretboard. At first, you practice with the game showing you exactly where each note is. Once you are comfortable with this, you use "Blind Fold" mode, where the game only shows where the first note is. Then, you have to use your ear to tell you where the rest are.

What else does a musical copycat game do? It trains your memory. The game forces you to quickly memorize a melody—a skill that will assist any guitar player, regardless of style.

INSTRUCTIONS

When you start Woody Says, you'll see a guitar fretboard and hear a melody play. As the melody plays, the location of the notes will light up. Simply echo back the notes that were played by clicking on the corresponding guitar frets. For example, if the melody consists of the second string, first fret, followed by second string, third fret, click on those two notes in that order. In the game, timing does not matter; only the order of pitches (notes) matters.

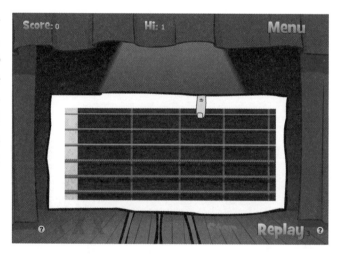

When the computer is playing the melody, the cursor is shaped like an ear. Should you need to stop playback, click on the "Stop" button. Or, if you need to hear the melody again, click on "Replay." You are allowed three playbacks per melody. When it's your turn to enter the melody, the cursor is shaped like a finger. The game continues until you make three mistakes on a single melody. The mistakes are shown by the red "X"s in the bottom left-hand corner.

All the melodies are four measures long. If you make it to the end of the melody, you receive a bonus and a new melody begins.

SETTINGS

Woody Says has several settings available. The difficulty of the game is controlled by the level box on the opening screen: one being easiest and ten the most difficult. In level one, a simple melody in C major is played. By level ten, the melody is *atonal* (not belonging to any one key) and very challenging. Woody Says can also be played with an onscreen piano keyboard instead of the guitar fretboard. (Basic familiarity with the piano keyboard is a must for any musician.)

For developing your musical ear, Woody Says can be played in "Blind Fold" mode. In this mode, the game only shows the location of the first note of the melody. For the rest of the notes, you need to figure out where they are by ear. This is difficult! If you miss in "Blind Fold" mode, the game will show you where the notes were on your next turn, so you don't have to keep guessing. "Blind Fold" mode is great for ear training. All players should make it their goal to eventually play the game in "Blind Fold" mode.

To do:

Get really good at levels one through three, then go back and play them in "Blind Fold" mode. Any score above 300, and you are among the greats.

END USER LICENSE AGREEMENT FOR GUITAR GAMES CD-ROM

END-USER LICENSE AGREEMENT FOR GUITAR GAMES IMPORTANT PLEASE READ THE TERMS AND CONDITIONS OF THIS LICENSE AGREEMENT CAREFULLY BEFORE USING THE GUITAR GAMES CD-ROM: William Wilson's End-User License Agreement ("EULA") is a legal agreement between you (either an individual or a single entity) and William Wilson for the software product(s) identified above which may include associated software components, media, printed materials, and "online" or electronic documentation ("Guitar Games"). By using Guitar Games, you agree to be bound by the terms of this EULA. This license agreement represents the entire agreement concerning the program between you and William Wilson, (referred to as "licenser"), and it supersedes any prior proposal, representation, or understanding between the parties. If you do not agree to the terms of this EULA, do not install or use Guitar Games.

Guitar Games is protected by copyright laws and international copyright treaties, as well as other intellectual property laws and treaties. Guitar Games Software is licensed, not sold.

1. GRANT OF LICENSE.
Guitar Games is licensed as follows:

(a) Installation and Use.

William Wilson grants you the right to use your copy of Guitar Games on your computer running a validly licensed copy of the operating system for which Guitar Games was designed [e.g. Windows XP, Windows Vista, etc.].

2. DESCRIPTION OF OTHER RIGHTS AND LIMITATIONS.
(a) Maintenance of Copyright Notices.

You must not remove or alter any copyright notices on any and all copies of Guitar Games.

(b) Distribution.

You may not distribute copies of the Guitar Games to third parties.

(c) Prohibition on Reverse Engineering, Decompilation, and Disassembly.

You may not reverse engineer, decompile, or disassemble Guitar Games, except and only to the extent that such activity is expressly permitted by applicable law notwithstanding this limitation.

(d) Rental.

You may not rent, lease, or lend Guitar Games.

(e) Support Services.

William Wilson will not provide support services for Guitar Games.

(f) Compliance with Applicable Laws.

You must comply with all applicable laws regarding use of Guitar Games.

3. TERMINATION
Without prejudice to any other rights, William Wilson may terminate this EULA if you fail to comply with the terms and conditions of this EULA. In such event, you must destroy all copies of Guitar Games in your possession.

4. COPYRIGHT
All title, including but not limited to copyrights, in and to Guitar Games and any copies thereof are owned by William Wilson or his suppliers. All title and intellectual property rights in and to the content which may be accessed through use of Guitar Games is the property of the respective content owner and may be protected by applicable copyright or other intellectual property laws and treaties. This EULA grants you no rights to use such content. All rights not expressly granted are reserved by William Wilson.

5. NO WARRANTIES
William Wilson expressly disclaims any warranty for Guitar Games. Guitar Games is provided "as is" without any express or implied warranty of any kind, including but not limited to any warranties of merchantability, non-infringement, or fitness of a particular purpose. William Wilson does not warrant or assume responsibility for the accuracy or completeness of any information, text, graphics, links, or other items contained within Guitar Games. William Wilson makes no warranties respecting any harm that may be caused by the transmission of a computer virus, worm, time bomb, logic bomb, or other such computer program. William Wilson further expressly disclaims any warranty or representation to Authorized Users or to any third party.

6. LIMITATION OF LIABILITY
In no event shall William Wilson be liable for any damages (including, without limitation, lost profits, business interruption, or lost information) rising out of 'Authorized Users' use of or inability to use Guitar Games, even if William Wilson has been advised of the possibility of such damages. In no event will William Wilson be liable for loss of data or for indirect, special, incidental, consequential (including lost profit), or other damages based in contract, tort or otherwise. William Wilson shall have no liability with respect to the content of Guitar Games or any part thereof, including but not limited to errors or omissions contained therein, libel, infringements of rights of publicity, privacy, trademark rights, business interruption, personal injury, loss of privacy, moral rights, or the disclosure of confidential information.